READING 2B
HEARTS AND HANDS

THIRD EDITION

bju **press**®

Greenville, South Carolina

NOTE:
The fact that materials produced by other publishers may be referred to in this volume does not constitute an endorsement of the content or theological position of materials produced by such publishers. Any references and ancillary materials are listed as an aid to the student or the teacher and in an attempt to maintain the accepted academic standards of the publishing industry.

READING 2B, Third Edition
Hearts and Hands

Project Authors
Dottie Buckley
Kathleen Hynicka
Amy Schoneweis

Bible Integration
Bryan Smith

Project Editor
Debbie L. Parker

Project Coordinator
Michele White

Design Coordinator
Duane Nichols

Page Layout
Maribeth Hayes

Art Director
Elly Kalagayan

Cover & Book Designer
Andrew Fields

Permissions
Sylvia Gass
Kathleen Thompson
Carrie Walker

Illustration Coordinator
Del Thompson

Illustrators
Paula Cheadle
Zach Franzen
Preston Gravely
Frank Ordaz
Kathy Pflug
John Roberts
Lynda Slattery
Courtney Wise

Art Technical Consultant
John Cunningham

Photograph credits appear on page 220.

Acknowledgments:

"Mice" from FIFTY-ONE NEW NURSERY RHYMES by Rose Fyleman. Used by permission of The Society of Authors as the Literary Representative of the Estate of Rose Fyleman. (45)

THANK YOU, AMELIA BEDELIA. Text copyright © 1964, 1993 by Peggy Parish. Illustrations copyright © 1964 by Fritz Siebel. Illustrations copyright renewed 1992 by the Estate of Fritz Siebel. Revised illustrations copyright © 1993 by the Estate of Fritz Siebel. Used by permission of HarperCollins Publishers. (63–87)

THE PUPPY WHO WANTED A BOY by Jane Thayer. Text copyright © 1958 by Catherine Woolley. Illustrations copyright © 1985 by Lisa McCue. Used by permission of HarperCollins Publishers. (158–88)

READING 2A, 2B, 2C, and 2D, Third Edition, were originally published as READING 2A, *If Skies Be Blue*, and READING 2B, *When the Sun Rides High*, Second Edition.

ISBN: 978-1-60682-197-8

15 14 13 12 11 10 9 8 7 6 5

CONTENTS

HEARTS AND HANDS

Characters

We learn about each character in a story in three ways.

1. how each character **looks**
2. what each character **says**
3. what each character **does**

• How are the children in each picture alike?

• How are they different from each other?

SOMEONE MY AGE

Realistic fiction by Milly Howard
illustrated by Lynda Slattery

Think as You Read

Who are the two main characters in the story?

How are the two main characters alike? How are they different?

3

Chloe Wants a Friend

"Mother, may I go and jump rope with Abby?" asked Sophia.

"Yes," Mother smiled.

"May I get my bike out and go riding with Matt?" asked James.

"Yes," answered Mother, "but be careful to watch for cars."

Chloe went outside and sat on the steps. Mother came and sat beside her.

"Sophia has a friend who lives in Apartment 28, and James has a friend who lives in Apartment 32. I'm the only one who doesn't have a friend that lives close by," said Chloe.

"You have a lot of friends at school," said Mother. "Why don't you ask one of them to come home with you on Friday? She could stay for supper too."

"That is not the same as having a friend who lives close to me," sighed Chloe.

"Well," Mother said, "a new family will soon be moving into Apartment 48. I met the Parks when they came to see about renting the apartment. Someone your age was with them. Maybe she will be your friend."

Chloe looked up at Mother and smiled. Mother gave her a big hug. "Why don't you skate awhile?" she said.

Chloe ran to get her skates. Mother helped her
put them on, and off Chloe skated. She waved
as she skated past Sophia and her friend, Abby,
skipping rope.

James and his friend, Matt, rode their bikes past
Chloe. She waved at them too.

Chloe was skating back towards her home when a van drove up to the apartments and stopped. Chloe stopped and watched as the van backed up to Apartment 48.

Chloe skated a little closer. She could see a man and a woman taking a small, round table and some plants into the apartment. She could see them taking in one box after another. Chloe's eyes opened wide when she saw the man lift a bike from the back of the van. "That bike looks just like mine!" she exclaimed to herself.

Someone Chloe's Age

When Chloe saw the bike that looked just like her bike, she skated even closer to Apartment 48.

The woman looked up and saw Chloe. "Hello," she said. "I am Mrs. Park. Who are you?"

"I am Chloe Stevens, and I'm seven," replied Chloe. "Do you have someone my age?"

Mrs. Park smiled. "Yes, Jin is inside helping." She turned and called into the apartment, "Come here, Jin. There's someone here to meet you."

Jin walked slowly through the doorway. She stopped and looked at Chloe.

"Hello," said Chloe.

Jin just smiled. Then she went back inside her apartment.

"Jin is shy," explained Mrs. Park. "Give her more time. She would like to have a friend. Come back and visit us soon."

"I will," said Chloe, and she skated home.

When Chloe got home, Mother was fixing dinner. She looked at Chloe and smiled. "Did you see someone your age?" asked Mother.

"Yes," Chloe said as she put her skates away. "Her name is Jin. I spoke to her, but she did not speak to me."

"Maybe she didn't hear you," said Mother.

"Oh, she heard me," Chloe said. "But Jin is shy."

"Why don't you try speaking to Jin every time you see her? You could ask her to go with you to Sunday school," Mother said.

And that is what Chloe did.

Often she skated past Apartment 48. Often she spoke to Jin.

"Would you like to go to Sunday school with me?" Chloe would ask.

"No, thank you," Jin would reply.

One day Jin was sitting on her steps when Chloe skated by. Jin was holding a pair of skates in her hands.

Chloe stopped and asked, "Can you skate?"

"Not yet," answered Jin.

"It's not hard," said Chloe. "You just take one step, then two steps, and then you slide. Let me help you."

Chloe helped Jin put on her skates. Then Chloe held Jin's hand and skated beside her. At first, Jin wobbled from side to side, but she kept on skating. When at last she stopped to rest, Jin asked, "Do you still go to Sunday school?"

"Yes," said Chloe. "Would you like to go with me?"

"Yes, and Mother said that I could go. Will you stop for me Sunday?" asked Jin.

"Yes," Chloe said with a smile.

Chloe hummed as she skated home. "Thank you, Lord," she said. "You gave me a friend that lives close by, someone who is just my age!"

"Someone My Age"

1. Who are the two main characters in the story?

2. How are Chloe and Jin alike?

3. How are Chloe and Jin different?

4. Why does Jin finally decide to go to Sunday school?

Vocabulary

apartment   exclaimed   renting

Write It

Write a paragraph about you and a friend. Think about how the two of you are alike and how you are different from each other. Write about how you are alike and how you are different.

Rhyming Words

Rhyming words are words that end with the same vowel and consonant sounds.

name	know
same	go

Welcome

Poetry by Rose Waldo
illustrated by Courtney Wise

Little new neighbor, have you come to be
A playmate of mine from over the sea?
I'm glad you are here. Oh, won't it be fine
To learn all your games, and I'll teach you mine!
We won't understand all the words that we say,
But I'm sure that we both will know how to play.
So will you come now and swing while I swing,
And we'll sing all the songs that we love to sing.

ok, puedo quedarme hasta
las 10:15

Where Are We?

Setting: Where a story takes place

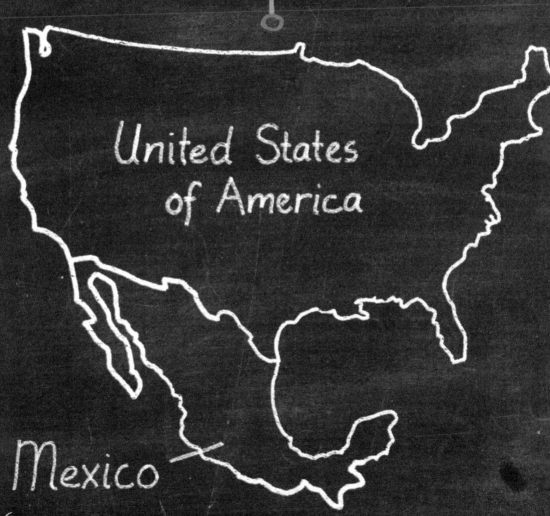

Realistic fiction by Milly Howard
illustrated by Zach Franzen

Think as You Read

Where does the story take place?

What problem do the new friends have?

Kristy and Ana

It was Ana's first day of school in America. She sat at her desk and watched the boys and girls. They laughed and talked quietly all around her. Ana sighed. She could understand only a few words in English. She knew the American children would not understand her Spanish.

"Hi!" said a pretty girl with curly red hair.

Ana knew that word. "Hi!" she replied, smiling.

The girl began talking. Ana just shook her head. "I no speak English," she said.

The girl looked puzzled.

Just then Mr. Mullins said that it was time to begin. Everyone stood to say the pledge to the American flag. Ana stood up tall and proud with her hand over her heart. She could not say the pledge yet, but America was her new country. She was glad to go to school and planned to work hard to learn English.

The class said the pledges to the Christian flag and to the Bible. Then Mr. Mullins prayed. Ana silently thanked God for her new Christian school.

Mr. Mullins spoke to the class in English. He called Ana's name and held up some books and supplies for her. Ana hurried to the front of the class to get them. As she carried them to her desk, the girl with the curly red hair smiled at her. Then Mr. Mullins began to teach the class.

For a little while Ana looked at the bright pictures in her schoolbooks. Then Mr. Mullins came to her desk. He handed Ana a paper with some math problems on it and said something to the redheaded girl. She pulled her chair up next to Ana's.

"Ana," Mr. Mullins said, "this is Kristy."

"Kristy?" Ana asked, looking at the girl.

"Yes, my name is Kristy," the girl said. She showed Ana the math work the class was doing. Soon Ana was busy working too. She quickly finished all of the problems on her paper. "Done," she said.

"Good!" Kristy exclaimed.

Ana nodded. "Sí," she said.

Kristy and Ana worked together the rest of the morning.

"It is time for lunch," Kristy said at last.

"Time? Lunch?" Ana repeated.

"Sí!" Kristy pretended to eat a sandwich.

Ana laughed. She understood that. She picked up her lunchbox and followed Kristy.

The two girls washed their hands with soap and water at the sink. Then they went to the lunchroom.

That afternoon Mr. Mullins handed out music books to the class. "Our school program is only two weeks away," he said. "We have learned many of the songs, but we still have a lot of work to do."

Ana liked to hear the class sing, and she knew some of the songs in Spanish. Mr. Mullins asked her to sing one to the class.

"Would you like to sing Ana's song in the program?" Mr. Mullins asked the class.

"Yes, sir!" was the answer.

Next they worked on Bible verses. Mr. Mullins wrote a verse for Ana to learn. Then he read the verse very slowly to her. Ana looked at the strange English words.

Mr. Mullins read the verse again, one phrase at a time. Ana repeated each phrase, but she did not think she would ever remember the words.

"I'll help you learn the verse," Kristy said.

Another Friend

Kristy helped Ana with her verse. Ana's mother also helped. She explained the verse in Spanish, and Ana said it in Spanish too.

One night Kristy came to Ana's house for dinner. Ana's mother made tortillas for tacos. Ana showed Kristy how to put the meat, beans, cheese, and tomatoes on the tortillas. Then she showed Kristy how to squeeze lime juice on top.

Ana put hot salsa on her tacos. Kristy tasted a little bit of the hot salsa. She said it burned her mouth. So she chose to put mild salsa on her tacos.

Ana's mother made something special called flan for dessert. It tasted like sweet pudding covered with caramel.

After dinner Ana tried to say her verse to Kristy. "1 John 4:19, 'We love Him, be . . . be . . .'" she stumbled.

"'Because He first loved us,'" Kristy said.

"'Because He first loved us,'" Ana repeated.

They finished just before Kristy's father came to take her home. "Good night, Ana," Kristy said.

Ana waved from the doorway. Maybe she would know her verse tomorrow.

On Saturday Ana played in the park.

"1 John 4:19, 'We love Him,' " she said as the swing went up. " 'Because He first loved us,' " she said as the swing came down.

A girl on the swing next to Ana listened to the words. "What are you saying?" she asked.

Ana gulped. Did the girl want her to say the Bible verse? Maybe the girl did not know that Jesus loved her and had died for her sins. Ana remembered the verse, but was she brave enough to say it to the girl?

Ana took a deep breath. " 'We love him, because he first loved us,' " she said.

"What does that mean?" the girl asked.

Ana thought of all the English words she had learned. Could she explain why she loved Jesus?

"Ana!" a voice called.

Ana turned around. "Kristy!" she said.

Kristy came running up to the swings. "Tell what 1 John 4:19 means," Ana said, pointing to the other girl.

"I'm Kristy, and this is Ana."

"I'm Sarah," the other girl said.

"Tell what 1 John 4:19 means," Ana repeated.

Kristy explained, "God loves us and wants to forgive us for doing wrong. We love Jesus because He died on the cross to save us from our sins. If you ask Him, He will forgive you too." Ana listened carefully. She wanted to know how to tell others about Jesus in English.

"We're going to say the verse and sing songs in a program at our school. Want to come?" asked Kristy.

"I don't know. Maybe," Sarah said.

"Okay," said Kristy. "Want to go down the slide?"

The days passed quickly. Every day Ana and Kristy prayed for Sarah. Every day Ana said her verse to Kristy.

The night of the program, Ana's class marched out proudly. When it was time to say the Bible verses, Ana looked at the crowd. Sarah was sitting in the front row! She smiled at Ana. Ana almost waved at her.

"1 John 4:19, 'We love Him, because He first loved us.'" Ana smiled. She had said the verse perfectly.

After the program, Ana found Kristy. Very carefully Ana said, "Thank you for helping me. You are a kind friend."

"You're welcome," Kristy said. "De nada!"

Ana laughed. "Go see Sarah," she said. "Over there."

"New Friends"

1. What problem did Ana and Kristy have?

2. Who helped Ana with her problem? How did they help Ana?

3. How would the story have been different if it had taken place in Mexico?

4. What should you do if you have a friend who needs to hear about Jesus?

Vocabulary

caramel	pledge	Spanish
dessert	pretended	tacos
phrase	salsa	tortillas

Life in a New Country

1 Juan 4:19

Nosotros le amamos a él, porque él nos amó primero.

"Oh, Dios es bueno"

Oh, Dios es bueno,
Oh, Dios es bueno,
Oh, Dios es bueno,
Dios es bueno para mí.

When Did It Happen?

Setting: When and where a story takes place

THE FIRE KEEPER

Realistic fiction by Milly Howard
illustrated by Preston Gravely

Think as You Read

When and where does the story take place?
What problems does the main character have?

The Fire

The smoke from the fire curled around Little Fox's head. He choked and fanned the smoke away. "Just once I wish I could go on a hunt with Father and the other men," he said.

White Cloud, Little Fox's mother, looked up from her bed of animal skins. She smiled at the small boy crouched over the fire.

"Then who would take care of me, Little Fox?" White Cloud asked. "Who would keep the fire going?"

Little Fox smiled back at his mother. Then, using a stick, he poked at the fire to make the orange flames burn more brightly. "I will keep the fire going, Mother. But soon you will be well. You will not need me to take care of you."

White Cloud moved her hurt leg under the animal skins. Little Fox looked up as she moaned. "I should have gone with you to the spring," he said. "I would have killed that wild pig! Then he would not have hurt you."

Little Fox grabbed a spear that was leaning against the wall of the cave. He thrust the spear toward a shadow. "There! He is dead!" Little Fox pretended. Then he put the spear back against the wall.

White Cloud laughed at the boy. Little Fox was glad to hear her laughter for he knew how much she suffered. White Cloud could not stand on her leg. So Shining Star, Little Fox's older sister, had gone to fetch water from the spring.

Little Fox sighed and picked up a small stone. His father and the other men had gone on the hunt two days ago. Little Fox wanted to go hunting with them, but all the men thought he was too little. All he could do was stay home and take care of the fire. He felt the edge of the stone. "It's sharp enough," thought Little Fox. He began to scratch on the wall of the cave, moving the sharp stone back and forth.

White Cloud saw the four legs of a buffalo appear. Then came the buffalo's back and its head. Soon the buffalo's eyes looked down at her from the wall. "How Little Fox can draw!" she thought. "Soon he will be old enough to go hunting with the men. He will hunt the animals he draws so well." White Cloud closed her eyes and lay back on the bed.

Little Fox mixed red clay with water and picked up a brush. He had made the brush himself using fur and a stick. Carefully he painted the buffalo red.

The fire flickered as he dug out burned sticks to mix with water and make black paint. "I'll add more branches to the fire soon," Little Fox said to himself, "but I'll finish my buffalo first."

He frowned at the stone bowl. There was not a drop of water left. "What is taking Shining Star so long?" he wondered. "She should be back with the water."

Little Fox walked to the mouth of the cave. All he could see were the treetops. He turned back to his painting.

"There is no water to make paint," Little Fox thought. "I'll draw with the burned tips of the sticks." Slowly he rubbed the sticks over the buffalo. He added a little black here and rubbed some out there. Then he stepped back to look.

"There! It's done!" he said to himself. "Now it looks more like a real buffalo."

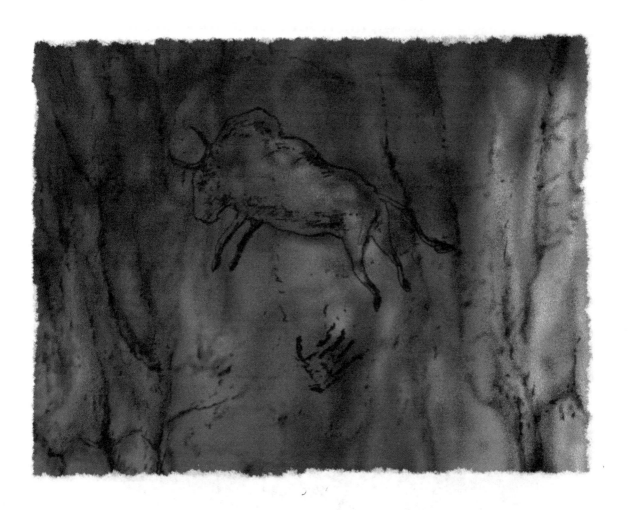

Mountain Lion

"Little Fox!"

Little Fox dropped the burned stick and ran to the mouth of the cave. Shining Star scrambled up the last few feet and stumbled past her brother.

"Mountain lion!" Shining Star gasped, pointing down the side of the cliff. Little Fox could see the mountain lion leaping from rock to rock up the side of the mountain.

"What is it?" called their mother, trying to sit up. Shining Star ran to White Cloud's side. "A mountain lion!" Shining Star cried.

"Use the fire to frighten him away!" White Cloud called to Little Fox.

Little Fox reached to grab a burning branch to frighten the mountain lion. But the fire had gone out!

The mountain lion leaped over the last few rocks and landed in the mouth of the cave. There it crouched, snarling!

Little Fox felt for the spear leaning against the wall of the cave. His fingers closed around the spear. His mouth was dry. This was no game. The mountain lion was no shadow to kill!

Little Fox yelled as loudly as he could. He ran at the mountain lion and threw the spear. Surprised, the mountain lion stepped back. It lost its footing and slid down a few feet. The spear flew over the mountain lion's head. Then Little Fox heard shouts below. The hunters were home!

The mountain lion turned quickly, leaped from the rocks, and was gone. Little Fox stood still as his father climbed into the cave.

"I let the fire go out, Father." Little Fox hung his head. "I didn't think keeping the fire was as important as hunting."

His father looked at Little Fox's bent head. "You were wrong to let the fire go out, Little Fox. You are the fire keeper. What would we do without our fire? Our fire warms us, and it protects us. But you were brave today, Little Fox. You will be a good hunter when you are a little older."

Little Fox lifted his head. His eyes brightened. "You forgive me?" he whispered.

"Yes," his father replied. "But you must be the fire keeper until the hunt is over."

"Oh, I will, Father!" Little Fox cried. "I'll keep the fire burning!" He ran to tend the fire and soon had it burning brightly.

That night Little Fox mixed his paints carefully. Before long a mountain lion glared down from the wall of the cave. The mountain lion's yellow eye glowed in the light of the fire. From then on, every time Little Fox looked at the mountain lion, he remembered to tend the fire.

"The Fire Keeper"

1. When does the story take place? How do you know?

2. Who is the main character? What problems did he have?

3. Discuss why obedience is important.

4. How would the story be different if Little Fox and his family lived in a house like your family lives in?

5. Discuss important jobs that you are asked to do in your home.

Vocabulary

buffalo	moaned	suffered
crouched	scrambled	
glared	snarling	

Rhythm

Rhythm: a repeated pattern of beats or sounds

ticktock, ticktock

choo choo, choo choo

march, march, march, march

Mice

Poetry by Rose Fyleman
illustrated by Kathy Pflug

I think mice
Are rather nice.

Their tails are long.
Their faces small.
They haven't any
Chins at all.
Their ears are pink,
Their teeth are white,
They run about
The house at night.
They nibble things
They shouldn't touch,
And no one seems
To like them much.

But I think mice
Are nice.

Mother Mouse

Millicent
(Milly)

Mortimer
(Morty)

Merry Mouse Thinks

Meredith
(Merry)

Fantasy by Eileen M. Berry
illustrated by Courtney Wise

Think as You Read

What could happen in real life?

Three Mice Go Hunting

The Mouse family lived in the attic in the home of Mrs. Theodora P. Claxton. Mother Mouse had three children—Millicent, Mortimer, and Meredith. They were called Milly, Morty, and Merry for short.

One day Mother said, "Children, it is going to rain. Remember what happened the last time it rained?"

Morty pointed to the hole in the wall. It was a hole about the size of a large marble, but to the mice it seemed huge. "Water came in through that big hole," he said.

"Our rug got soaking wet," said Milly.

"There was a puddle on the kitchen floor," said Merry. She remembered that puddle best of all. It had been great fun to scamper back and forth through it, but Mother had not been happy. Merry had soaked her tail in the water and waved it around like a water sprinkler. Water sprayed all over the kitchen, and the cheese sandwiches on the table were soggy.

"Merry," Mother had said with her paws on her hips, "before you act, think of others. Are you making life easy or hard for them?"

Merry had to wipe up every drop with a scrap of paper towel. She had not forgotten.

Now Mother frowned at the hole in the wall. "We do not want water coming in again. We need to find something to plug the hole."

Milly's face lit up with excitement. "May we go down into the house and hunt for something?" she squeaked. She folded her paws together under her chin. "Please?"

Mother's eyes moved from Milly to Morty to Merry. They rested on Merry. "I'm glad you want to help," she said. "Yes, you may go. But be careful. Stay away from mousetraps. And above all, you must stay away from the cat. Do you understand?"

Milly, Morty, and Merry nodded their heads.

Mother kissed each one in turn. "Be safe," she said, "and be back before supper."

The door to the attic opened into Mrs. Claxton's coat closet. The three mice scrambled down the rope pull and swung onto the closet rod. Then they scurried down the slippery sleeve of a raincoat and dropped to the floor.

"Where should we go first?" asked Morty.

Milly was the oldest and the most careful. "Let's go to the sewing room," she said. "Mrs. Claxton will not be there right now. She will be having tea in the sitting room."

"Keep to the shadows," said Morty as the three mice scampered along the hall.

The mice stopped in the doorway of the sewing room. A basket sat on the floor beside the rocking chair. "There's Mrs. Claxton's sewing basket!" Merry squealed. "It's sure to have yarn or scraps of cloth we could use."

"Shhh." Milly put her paw over Merry's mouth. "Keep your voice down, Merry."

They crept toward the basket. Suddenly Morty stopped short. He pointed to the rocking chair. Curled on the seat lay Snowball, Mrs. Claxton's white cat. Her eyes were closed. Her sides moved in and out with her deep, slow breathing.

"She's asleep," whispered Merry.

"Yes, but the sewing basket is too close to her," said Milly. "She might hear us and wake up. Let's go."

The mice turned and scurried out of the room. At the door Merry looked back. Snowball opened one eye lazily. Then she closed it again.

"Let's try the bathroom," said Morty. "I remember seeing cotton balls in there."

Three Mice for Tea

The cotton balls were in a glass jar on the high sink. The mice tried to climb the pipes. They slipped and slid, and they slid and slipped. At last they all landed in a pile on the floor.

"It's no use," said Morty. "We'll never get up there."

"Let's think," said Milly. "What else could we use to plug the hole?"

"How about newspaper?" asked Morty. "Mrs. Claxton won't mind if we take a page. She always says there's no good news in the paper anyway."

"Where does Mrs. Claxton keep the newspaper?" asked Merry.

"In the sitting room," said Milly. "And that's where she's having tea."

"We'll just have to be very quiet," said Morty. "Come on. Let's go."

As they neared the sitting room, the mice heard voices and clinking teacups. "Oh dear," said Milly. "Mrs. Claxton has company for tea. I don't feel good about this."

Morty peeked around the doorway. "They're seated at the tea table over by the window," he said. "Mrs. Claxton and two other ladies."

"Can you see any newspapers?" asked Merry.

"There's one on the sofa near us," said Morty. "Let's be quick and quiet."

The three mice ran up the leg of the sofa and leaped onto a soft pillow. They tugged at a page of the newspaper.

Suddenly Mrs. Claxton stood and walked toward them. "Zelda, I just saw an ad for that new cat food in the paper today," she said. "I'll tear it out for you."

The three mice dove between the pages of the newspaper. They froze.

"It's right here, Zelda, on the back page by the crossword puzzle." Mrs. Claxton picked up the paper and opened it. "Eeeeeaaaak!" She screamed and threw the paper across the room. "Help! Mice! Help!"

The three mice landed with a thump on the floor by the tea table. Mrs. Claxton's two friends shrieked and climbed up onto their chairs.

"Snowball!" Mrs. Claxton screamed. "Snowball, come quick! Catch these nasty critters!"

"Back to the attic!" Milly cried. "This way—now!"

Milly scampered off toward the doorway. Morty followed right on Milly's tail, but Merry stopped still in her tracks. Something had caught her eye.

Underneath the tea table lay a crumpled paper napkin. It was covered with pink and red roses. It was beautiful. It would be perfect for plugging the hole.

Mother's words came back to Merry's mind. "Before you act, think of others."

Merry scampered under the tea table and snatched up the napkin in her teeth. Then she ran for the doorway, but she was too late. Mrs. Claxton stood right in Merry's way with the rolled-up newspaper in her hand. And just behind Mrs. Claxton was Snowball.

Merry stopped for only a moment. Then she ran as fast as she could toward Mrs. Claxton's shiny black shoes.

"I'm going to faint!" Mrs. Claxton wobbled backwards, stepping on Snowball's paw. Snowball howled. Merry streaked past them. She raced down the hall and into the closet. She jumped onto the belt of the raincoat and scrambled up the sleeve.

Milly and Morty were waiting. "Up the rope pull, Merry—hurry!"

The three mice tumbled back into the attic and lay panting. Merry dropped the napkin at Mother's feet.

"It's beautiful!" Milly said.

"It will plug up the hole," said Morty.

"It's perfect," Mother said. She gave Merry a hug. "My dear girl! It was foolish for you to get so close to Mrs. Claxton. And it was very foolish for you to get so close to the cat. But thank you for thinking of me. This napkin will make my life easier."

"Merry Mouse Thinks"

1. What in the story could have happened in real life?

2. What in the story could not have happened in real life?

3. What lesson did Merry Mouse learn?

4. What can you do to show that you think about others first?

Vocabulary

attic	faint	sewing
company	moment	shrieked
else	scamper	sofa
excitement	scurried	

Keep the Beat

> **Rhythm**: a repeated pattern of beats or sounds

Think of words to complete the poem.
Be sure to keep the beat!

Mousy Fun

Merry and Morty and Milly
Did something a little bit silly.
They knew that the ___ would be sleeping,
So all through the ___ they went creeping.
Milly and ___ and Morty
Did something a little bit sporty.
They ___ down a hill of potatoes,
And ___ a pile of tomatoes.

What Does It Mean?

Sometimes words or phrases have two different meanings.

Pick up your room.

Thank You, Amelia Bedelia

Fiction by Peggy Parish
illustrated by Barbara Siebel Thomas

Think as You Read

What are the words and phrases that Amelia Bedelia does not understand?

Mrs. Rogers was all in a dither. "Great-Aunt Myra is coming today."

"Now, that is nice," said Amelia Bedelia. "I do love company."

"We've been trying for years to get her to visit," said Mrs. Rogers, "but Great-Aunt Myra says the only place she feels at home is at home. So everything must be exactly right. We do want her to be happy here."

"Now don't you worry your head," said Amelia Bedelia. "I'll fix everything. What should I do first?"

"Well, the guest room must be made ready. Strip the sheets off the bed. Remake it with the new rosebud sheets," said Mrs. Rogers. "Thank goodness you're here."

Amelia Bedelia went to the guest room. "These folks do have odd ways. Imagine stripping sheets after you use them." Amelia Bedelia shook her head. But she stripped those sheets.

Amelia Bedelia had just finished when the
doorbell rang. "That must be the laundryman with
Mr. Rogers's shirts," called Mrs. Rogers. "Please
check them and make sure they're all there."

Amelia Bedelia hurried to the door and took the
package. Amelia Bedelia opened the package. She
unfolded each shirt.

"Two sleeves, one collar, one pocket, and six buttons. Yes, they're all here. There's not a thing missing," said Amelia Bedelia. "Now to check them. It would be a sight easier to buy them already checked," said Amelia Bedelia. But she quickly checked each shirt.

Mrs. Rogers came downstairs in a rush. "Amelia Bedelia, my bright pink dress has spots in it. Please remove them with this spot remover. Leave the dress out. I will wear it tonight. Now I must go to the market."

Amelia Bedelia looked at the bright pink
dress. "I don't see any spots. This dress just needs
washing." Then another dress caught Amelia
Bedelia's eye.

"She must have meant her light pink dress. Now
that one sure is spotted." Amelia Bedelia held the
dress up. "It looks mighty nice with the spots in it.
But I guess she's tired of it that way."

Amelia Bedelia put spot
remover on each spot. Then
she waited. Nothing happened.

"Didn't think that stuff would work," said
Amelia Bedelia. She got the scissors. And Amelia
Bedelia removed every spot from that dress.

"Amelia Bedelia," called Mrs. Rogers. "Please take these groceries."

Amelia Bedelia ran to take the bag.

"Here are some roses, too. Do scatter them around the living room. I must get my hair done now. While I'm gone, wash all the vegetables and string the beans. If you have time, make a jelly roll. Great-Aunt Myra does love jelly roll," said Mrs. Rogers.

Amelia Bedelia stopped in the living room.
"Seems like roses would look nicer sitting
proper-like in vases. But if she wants them
scattered, scattered they will be."

Amelia Bedelia went
on to the kitchen with the
groceries. She washed all
the vegetables.

Then she found a ball of
string. And Amelia Bedelia
strung all those beans.

73

"Jelly! Roll!" exclaimed Amelia Bedelia. "I never heard tell of jelly rolling." But Amelia Bedelia got out a jar of jelly. Amelia Bedelia tried again and again. But she just could not get that jelly to roll.

Amelia Bedelia washed her hands. She got out a mixing bowl. Amelia Bedelia began to mix a little of this and a pinch of that.

"Great-Aunt Myra or no Great-Aunt Myra—there's not going to be any rolling jelly in this house tonight," said Amelia Bedelia.

Mr. and Mrs. Rogers arrived home at the same time. Mrs. Rogers called, "Amelia Bedelia, please separate three eggs and pare the other vegetables you washed. I'll do the cooking." Then she and Mr. Rogers hurried upstairs to dress.

Amelia Bedelia took out three eggs. "I wonder why they need to be separated. They've been together all day and nothing happened." But Amelia Bedelia separated those eggs.

"Pair the vegetables!" Amelia Bedelia laughed.
"Here, you two go together—and you two. Now be
careful, or I'll be separating you, too."

Amelia Bedelia went up to Mrs. Rogers's room. "What should I do with these stripped sheets?" she asked. "Stripped sheets!" exclaimed Mrs. Rogers. But she got no further.

Mr. Rogers roared, "What in thunderation happened to my shirts?"

"Oh, don't you like big checks? I didn't have time to do little ones. But I will next time," promised Amelia Bedelia.

"My dress!" exclaimed Mrs. Rogers. "It's full of holes."

"Yes, ma'am, I removed every single spot," said Amelia Bedelia.

Before Mrs. Rogers could say any more, the doorbell rang.

"Great-Aunt Myra," said Mr. and Mrs. Rogers. They rushed to the front door.

"Good evening, grandniece. Good evening, grandnephew. My, that trip made me hungry," said Great-Aunt Myra.

"I'll cook dinner right now," said Mrs. Rogers.

Everybody went into the kitchen.

"Amelia Bedelia, did you string the beans?" asked Mrs. Rogers.

"Yes. See—they do give such a homey look," said Amelia Bedelia.

"Where are the eggs I asked you to separate?" said Mrs. Rogers.

"Here's one, one is behind the clock, and the other is over there. Did I separate them far enough apart?" asked Amelia Bedelia.

Mrs. Rogers said nothing. So Amelia Bedelia went on.

"And I paired the vegetables. They went together real well, and there weren't any left over."

Mrs. Rogers slapped her hand on the table. It hit right in a sticky blob. "Ugh! What is that?" she shouted.

"Jelly. I tried to make it roll. But it just plip-plopped all over the place," said Amelia Bedelia.

"Amelia Bedelia!" exclaimed Mrs. Rogers. "How do you get things so mixed up?"

"Things mixed up! Oh, I plumb forgot," said Amelia Bedelia. She hurried to the stove.

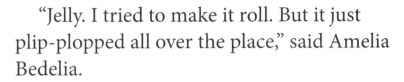

Amelia Bedelia opened the oven door.
Great-Aunt Myra sat up straight and sniffed.

"Hot apple pie! I do declare. Now that's the kind
of mixed-up thing I like."

Great-Aunt Myra announced, "Grandniece,
grandnephew, I like it here."

"Oh, Great-Aunt Myra, we're so glad!" said Mr.
and Mrs. Rogers.

They both began to talk at once. But Great-Aunt
Myra wasn't much for words. She had her eyes on
that last piece of pie.

Great-Aunt Myra put the last piece of pie on her plate. Then she said, "Grandniece, grandnephew, I will visit you often. That Amelia Bedelia really knows how to make a body feel at home. Thank you, Amelia Bedelia."

Amelia Bedelia smiled. She and Great-Aunt Myra would get along.

Thank You, Amelia Bedelia

1. Why was it hard for Amelia Bedelia to follow Mrs. Rogers's directions?

2. What were some of the directions Amelia Bedelia did not understand? Tell what Amelia Bedelia did when she tried to follow each direction.

3. Tell about a time that you were asked to follow directions that you did not understand.

4. What did Amelia Bedelia do that turned out to be just right?

Vocabulary

declare	grandniece	pare
dither	groceries	plumb
folks	laundryman	separate
grandnephew	ma'am	vegetables

Read as a Play

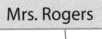

Mrs. Rogers

Amelia Bedelia

Narrator

Mr. Rogers and
Mrs. Rogers

"My dress!" exclaimed Mrs. Rogers. "It's full of holes."

"Yes, ma'am, I removed every single spot," said Amelia Bedelia.

Before Mrs. Rogers could say any more, the doorbell rang.

"Great-Aunt Myra," said Mr. and Mrs. Rogers. They rushed to the front door.

80

Cast

Amelia Bedelia

Mrs. Rogers

Mr. Rogers

Great-Aunt Myra

Narrator

The Braille Alphabet

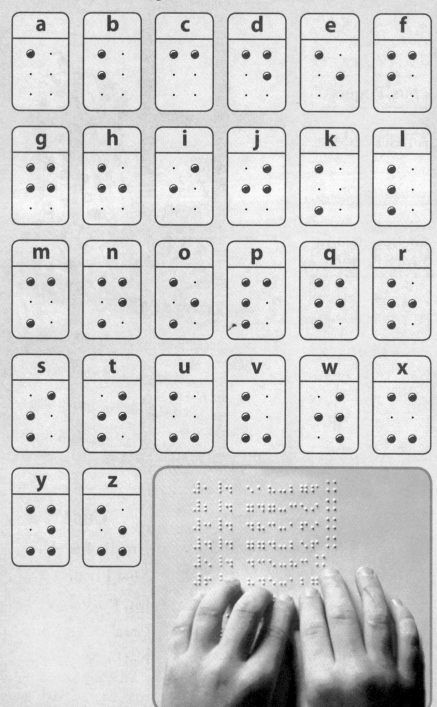

Annie Sullivan

April 14, 1886–October 20, 1936

Biography by Becky Davis and Eileen M. Berry
illustrated by Paula Cheadle

Think as You Read

Who is Annie Sullivan?

What special things does Annie learn and do?

Tewksbury

"What is this place?" Ten-year-old Annie Sullivan clutched her brother Jimmie's arm and squinted at the building in front of her. With her other hand she rubbed her red, puffy eyes. She hoped the man who had brought them here would not think she had been crying. Her eyes were swollen because of a sickness that had left her almost blind.

"This is Tewksbury," answered the man. "A home for the poor. You and your brother will be living here for a while."

92

Annie did not think much of Tewksbury. Many of the people there were old or sick. Like Annie and Jimmie, they all had no one to care for them. Annie stayed close to Jimmie. "I'll take care of you," she told him. Jimmie was lame, and the pain in his legs grew worse every day.

One morning Annie woke up and found that Jimmie's cot was gone. He had died during the night.

Annie spent days sitting still and staring at the empty space by her bed. She did not want to play. She did not even want to talk.

One day a girl about Annie's age walked over. "Would you like me to read to you?" the girl asked. Annie listened as her new friend read stories from books. Annie tried to see the pictures, but she saw only colored shapes. "I want to learn to read too," Annie thought.

Annie told her wishes to Miss Maggie, a lady in charge of Tewksbury. Miss Maggie thought for a moment. "I have heard of a school where they teach blind people to read. It's called Perkins. I have even read of a lady at Perkins who is  both blind and deaf. Laura Bridgman is her name. She has learned many things at the school." Miss Maggie's voice became sad. "But it costs money to go there. You don't have any money, Annie. You may as well face it. You will be at Tewksbury for the rest of your life."

"No, I won't," said Annie. "Somehow, I am going to go to that school, and I am going to learn to read."

The thought of school never left Annie's mind. One day some men came to inspect Tewksbury.

"This is your chance, Annie," whispered a friend. "One of those men is Mr. Sanborn. He knows about Perkins—that school for the blind."

As they were about to leave, Annie ran up to the men. "Mr. Sanborn!" she cried. "I want to learn to read! Please let me go to Perkins."

Annie was told to go back to her room. Weeks passed. Annie kept waiting and hoping. Then, one day Miss Maggie sent for her.

"Annie, I have wonderful news! This letter says that you can go to Perkins School for the Blind. You won't have to pay a cent!"

Perkins

September came. Annie rode a train to Perkins School for the Blind. She was almost fifteen years old, but the teachers put her in the first grade.

The other children in the first grade couldn't see Annie, but they knew she was much older than they were. "Big Annie! Big Annie!" they teased.

Annie gritted her teeth. "I'll put up with anything as long as I can learn to read," she said.

Because Annie's eyes were bad, she learned to read raised letters by feeling their shapes. She would sit and read for hours. She read stories of princes and giants. She read about great leaders in history and people in the Bible. "There's a whole new world inside books," Annie thought. "What would it be like to see the pictures?"

Not long before Annie finished school, a doctor tried an operation on her eyes. When the doctor removed the strips of cloth from her eyes, Annie held her breath. "Annie," the doctor asked, "can you see me?"

Annie opened her eyes. The doctor's face seemed to swim in the air. Then very slowly his face became clear.

"I can see you!" Annie whispered. She looked around the room. "I can see the nurse and the bed and the window. Not just shapes—the real things!" Annie gripped the sheet tightly. "It's better than any picture in a book."

Annie finished school in just six years. She began to think about what she should do next.

"I have a letter you might like to see," a friend at Perkins said to Annie one day. "The Keller family lives in Alabama. Their six-year-old daughter, Helen, can't see or hear. She needs a good teacher. Are you interested in the job?"

Annie frowned. How could she teach a girl who could not see or hear? Then Annie thought of Miss Bridgman, the blind and deaf lady at Perkins who had become her friend. People could "talk" to Miss Bridgman by spelling words into her hand with their fingers. Could Helen be taught in the same way?

Annie made her decision. "It will be a big job," she said, "but I'm willing to try."

Annie didn't have much to pack. A few days later she was on the train to Alabama. Annie stared out the window. She thought of little Helen Keller. *Clack-a-clack, clack-a-clack*, the wheels rattled below her. "*Blind and deaf, blind and deaf*," they seemed to say.

Annie said to herself, "I was blind too. I learned to read, and I know the finger alphabet. I'm sure I can help Helen to understand me. I'll do my best."

When Annie got to the Keller home, the first thing she saw was a little girl. The girl's hair was messy, and her dress was dirty. "So this is Helen," Annie thought. She gave Helen the doll she had brought for her.

Alabama

At supper Helen sat beside Annie. Annie watched as Helen's mother tried to get her to eat. Helen just threw her spoon and grabbed food off her mother's plate. Then she ran away from the table.

Annie went to find Helen. She laid the doll in Helen's arms. Then she spelled the word *d-o-l-l* into Helen's hand. Helen smiled.

When Annie tried to put the doll away, Helen became angry. She kicked Annie and hit Annie with her fists. "Before I can teach Helen," said Annie, "she must learn to obey."

Helen had never learned to obey. Her family felt sorry for her and had always let Helen do as she liked. Now Annie had an idea. "I must take Helen away from here," she said.

Helen's father let Annie take Helen to a little house nearby.

At first Annie had a hard time. Helen fought when Annie tried to dress her or put her to bed. Sometimes Annie wanted to get angry too. Sometimes she sat down and cried. But Annie kept trying. She never let Helen get her own way.

Slowly, Helen began to change. She stopped hitting, kicking, and fighting. She learned to be quiet when she did not get what she wanted. One day Helen even let Annie hold her on her lap.

"It's time we moved back to the big house," Annie told Helen's mother and father. "I think I can teach Helen, now that she knows she must obey."

Soon Helen learned how to repeat Annie's hand spellings with her fingers. But Annie could tell that Helen did not understand. She did not know that *d-o-l-l* meant the soft toy that she held in her arms. She did not know that *c-a-k-e* meant the food that tasted good. Every lesson was like a game to Helen. Annie often lay awake at night, thinking. "How will I ever make her understand?"

Months passed. One warm day, Annie and Helen went outside to the water pump for a drink. Helen put her mug under the water. As Annie always did, she spelled the word into Helen's hand. "*W-a-t-e-r, w-a-t-e-r,*" Annie spelled as the cool water gushed into the mug and over Helen's hands.

Suddenly, Helen dropped her mug and smiled. Her fingers quickly spelled the word back into Annie's hand. Helen spelled the word again and again. Something was different.

"She understands," Annie whispered. Then she looked up at the sky. "She understands!" Annie shouted. She laughed and threw her arms around Helen. "Oh, Helen, now you understand what words are. Now I can teach you to talk with your fingers just as well as anybody else can talk with his mouth."

Helen pointed to the pump. "*P-u-m-p*," Annie spelled into Helen's hand. Helen ran to a tree and pointed. "*T-r-e-e*," Annie spelled. Then Helen reached out and touched Annie. "*T-e-a-c-h-e-r*." Helen learned hundreds of new words that day.

At last, Annie Sullivan had freed Helen Keller from her dark, silent prison.

"Annie Sullivan"

1. Who is Annie Sullivan? What special things does Annie learn and do?

2. In what three places does the story take place? Why is each place important for Annie?

3. How does God want us to treat people who cannot see, hear, or walk?

Vocabulary

alphabet	lame
decision	operation
freed	prison
idea	squinted
inspect	swollen
interested	taught

Character Web

A **character web** is like a word web. A character web shows details about a character in a story. **Details** tell us what the character in a story is like.

learned to read

Helen Keller's teacher

had been almost blind

Annie Sullivan

?

Have You Seen My Dog?

Realistic fiction by Milly Howard
illustrated by Zach Franzen

Think as You Read

Who is the main character? What is he like?
What is the main character's dog like?

Where Is Lady?

Cole jumped down the porch steps and pushed open the gate to the backyard. "Here, Lady!" he called. There was no answering bark. The fenced yard was empty. Cole frowned. "That dog is gone again," he said.

Cole got his bike out of the shed and pushed it to the front yard. He stopped beside his father.

"Dad, have you seen Lady?" Cole asked.

"Why, no," said his father. "Is she gone again?"

"Yes, sir," Cole replied. "May I go look for her?"

"Yes," said his father. "Why don't you ask Alex to help you?"

Cole rode down the street to Alex's house. Alex was outside mowing the lawn. "Have you seen Lady?" Cole asked.

Alex stopped the lawn mower. "No, not this morning. Is she gone again?" he asked.

Cole nodded. "Lady has been wandering off since her puppies died. She must be looking for them."

"I'm almost done here," Alex said. "If you'll finish mowing this last bit of grass, I'll go ask Mom if I can help you look for Lady."

Cole finished the mowing. As he was putting away the lawn mower, Alex came running back with his bike. "Mom said it's okay. Let's go!"

The two boys headed up the street, but they didn't see Lady anywhere.

As they turned the corner of Maple Lane and Main Street, their friend Henry waved at them from his yard.

"Hi, Henry!" called Cole.

"What are you two doing?" Henry asked.

"We're looking for Lady," said Cole. "She got out again, and we can't find her anywhere."

"She ran past here early this morning," said Henry.

"Which way did she go?" Alex asked.

Henry pointed toward the lumberyard. "She headed out that way," he said.

"Thanks, Henry," called Cole and Alex as they rode away.

"Here, Lady!" Cole whistled for her as they rode up to the lumberyard.

Alex braked suddenly. "There she is!"

"Lady!" Cole called loudly. "Come here!"

The boys turned into the lumberyard. They rode in and out of the stacks of lumber, but they did not see Lady. They called and whistled, but there was no answer.

A tall man stopped them as they turned a corner. "What are you kids doing? You can't ride through here. This isn't a playground."

"We're sorry, sir," said Cole. "We're just looking for my dog."

The man put his hands on his hips and frowned. "A dog?"

"Yes, sir," said Alex. "I thought I saw her go around that corner."

"A dog about this big?" The man held his hands about knee high. "Brown, floppy ears, big brown eyes?"

"That's Lady!" exclaimed Alex.

"She went through a broken board in the back fence," the man replied. "There's a vacant lot over there."

"Thank you!" called the boys as they rode away. They rode their bikes down the side road to the vacant lot.

"Look," said Alex, pointing to an old shed almost hidden in the weeds.

A muffled bark came from the shed.

"Lady!" cried Cole. He got off his bike and ran the rest of the way to the shed door.

Lady looked up at the boys and wagged her tail. Then she nudged the squirming, furry bodies beside her.

"Puppies! Lady has puppies!" exclaimed Alex.

Cole dropped to his knees beside Lady. "Alex, these aren't puppies!"

113

Lady's New Family

"What are they?" Alex asked. He bent over to get a better look at the furry bodies. "You must be kidding!" He laughed. "Kittens!"

"Remember when Lady's puppies died?" Cole asked. "Lady wandered around the neighborhood for days looking for them. She must have found these kittens alone and adopted them."

"Something must have happened to their mother," said Alex. "I wonder. . ."

"So do I," Cole said.

Cole stroked Lady's head. "Well," he said at last, "we can take the kittens home in our bike crates. Lady will follow us."

Lady whimpered as the boys put the kittens into the crates. Then she ran beside the bikes all the way home.

"Mom! Dad!" Cole shouted as they turned into the driveway. "Come and see what we have!"

His mother and father came to the kitchen door. Cole and Alex put the kittens on the grass.

"How cute," said Mrs. Wei, picking up one of the kittens. "Where did you find them?"

"We didn't find them," said Alex. "Lady did."

"Lady found them?" Mr. Wei raised his eyebrows.

"Yes, sir. They were in an old shed near the lumberyard," said Alex.

"Where is their mother?" asked Mrs. Wei.

"We don't know," Cole replied. "Lady was taking care of them."

"You mean she adopted them?" asked Mr. Wei.

"Yes, sir," said Alex.

"I've heard of animals adopting other animals," said Mr. Wei. "But that doesn't happen very often."

Alex stood up suddenly. "Hey, Cole, why don't you call the newspaper office? This would make a good story."

Mrs. Wei carried the kittens inside. Cole and Alex raced for the phone.

By the time the newspaper reporter arrived, the kittens were well used to their new home. The reporter asked Cole and Alex some questions. Then she took pictures of Lady licking the kittens.

A few days later, Cole proudly showed the newspaper article to his classmates.

Almost every day after that, someone would knock at the kitchen door wanting to see Lady and her kittens. Cole enjoyed taking his friends to meet Lady. Each day the kittens grew bigger and bigger.

One day as Cole made a peanut butter sandwich at the kitchen counter, one little kitten sneaked up on him from behind. It made a flying leap.

"Peanut butter paw prints? On my kitchen counter?" asked his mother. She handed Cole a cloth.

There was a ripping sound behind them.

"My curtains!" his mother cried.

Mr. Wei took the kitten off the curtain. "I think it's time the kittens learned about the big outdoors," he said firmly.

Cole and his father took Lady and her kittens into the backyard. All went well for a few days. Then the neighborhood dogs discovered the kittens. The noise was awful! Even Cole put his hands over his ears.

"Sorry, Son," Cole's father said. "The kittens have got to go. You know we'll find good homes for them."

When Cole came home from school the next day, he ran to the backyard. He was not surprised to find that the kittens were gone. Lady lay in the grass, her head on her paws. She did not look up.

Cole stopped beside his father. "Dad, Lady sure looks lonely."

"Just watch," Mr. Wei replied. There was a slight movement on the doghouse roof. A small bundle of fur stretched and arched its back lazily. The kitten looked at the sad, lonely dog below and switched its tail back and forth. It sprang! "Woof!" barked the surprised dog.

Away dashed the kitten with Lady happily chasing it.

"We kept one for Lady," said Mr. Wei. "I think she'll have her paws full!"

"Have You Seen My Dog?"

1. Who is the main character in the story? What is he like?

2. What is Lady like?

3. Are Cole and Alex good friends? How do you know?

4. Tell about a time when you helped a friend.

Vocabulary

article	nudged	whimpered
awful	office	whistled
discovered	vacant	
lumber	wandering	

Write It

Think of someone you have helped. Write about who you helped and how you were helpful.

Looking for Details

Details help us learn about people, places, and things. Details also help us enjoy a story.

Cheerful Chickadees

Realistic fiction by Karen Wilt
illustrated by Kathy Pflug

Think as You Read

What can I learn about chickadees?

The Chickadee Feeder

"Let's go for a walk in the woods," said Dad. "Put on your coats and boots."

Mother handed Mark and Becky their hats and mittens. Then she waved goodbye as they started out. "Have fun," she called after them.

A Saturday walk in the woods with Dad was always fun. He showed Mark and Becky many things—foxes' dens, birds' nests, and rabbits' holes. They even saw raccoon tracks beside a frozen puddle of water.

"Look at that spruce tree," Dad said. "Maybe you'll see some good friends of mine." They all stopped talking. They stood still, looking at the tree.

Before long, one little bird began to twitter, "Chick-a-dee-dee-dee." Soon many birds around the tree began to twitter. They pecked at the seeds in the cones.

"Chickadees," Becky said. "All in their tiny black hoods."

"That black hood is part of their name," said Dad. "They are called black-capped chickadees."

"Look!" Mark whispered. "One of them is hanging upside down."

"They do that, but they never fall," Becky said.

"The chickadee is hunting for insects in the bark," Dad said.

After a while they walked on. Becky and Mark looked for more chickadees. They counted sixteen of them, but they heard many more calling "chick-a-dee-dee-dee" from the treetops.

At last they turned to go home. As they walked into the backyard, Mark pointed to a spruce tree. "We have chickadees in our own backyard," he exclaimed. "And look how fat they are!"

Dad chuckled. "Those chickadees have put on winter coats! As it gets colder they ruffle and puff out their feathers till they feel snug as can be. The feathers trap warm air next to their skin and keep the winter air out."

"Could we feed the chickadees?" Becky asked.

"I could make a bird feeder from a milk carton," Mark said.

"I think that's a great idea," Dad said.

127

At home Mark went right to work. He cut two openings in the sides of a milk carton. Dad helped Mark put a hook in the top of the feeder. Then Mark hung the feeder in a tree, and Becky put in some birdseed.

From the kitchen window Becky and Mark could peek at the feeder.

Chickadee Tamers

Many chickadees came to Becky and Mark's bird feeder. The birds twittered and ate the birdseed while Becky and Mark ate their oatmeal in the morning. The birds twittered and ate the birdseed while the children ate their sandwiches at lunch. But the chickadees ate the birdseed between meals too. Every day Becky had to put more birdseed in the feeder.

Sometimes Becky and Mark would sit in the yard when the chickadees came to the feeder. One day a chickadee sat on a branch of a nearby tree and looked at them. Mark whistled at it. The chickadee seemed to whistle back.

Dad came outside and sat down beside Becky and Mark. The chickadees fluttered back and forth in the yard. "Those chickadees have become tame," Dad said. "Do they land on your hand and take birdseed yet?"

"They would eat out of our hands?" Mark asked.

"They might," Dad answered.

Becky and Mark grabbed some birdseed and
stood close to the feeder. They waited and waited.
Then they heard a "chick-a-dee-dee-dee."

A chickadee fluttered in a circle around Mark. It
landed on his hand, took a seed, and then fluttered
away. Soon another chickadee came and took
one of Becky's seeds. It went to a tree and sang,
"Chick-a-dee-dee-dee."

After a little while, Mother called them in for hot apple cider. They all looked out the window to watch the birds. "It's snowing again," Mother said.

"What will happen to the chickadees?" Becky asked.

"God takes care of all the animals, Becky. He will take care of the chickadees," Dad said.

Mark smiled. "Dad, you said the chickadees ruffle and puff out their feathers to trap warm air next to their skin. Is that how God takes care of them?"

"Yes," Dad said, "God has given chickadees a way to protect themselves from the cold weather."

The snow fell all afternoon, but the chickadees twittered and played happily.

The snow kept falling all night.

The next morning Becky and Mark woke up to a bright white day. The snowstorm had stopped, and the sun had come out. The sun shining on the snow made it sparkle like glitter.

Becky and Mark dressed and ate. Then they went outside to clear away the snow. "If I were a giant, I would sneeze. Then all the snow would blow away!" Mark said.

Becky giggled. "But you are not a giant, Mark. We still have to clear away the snow."

Mark brushed off the car, and Becky cleared the walk. "I'll clear the snow off the bird feeder," Mark said. He dusted off the snow. "Where are the chickadees today?" he asked. "I hope they didn't freeze."

Just then the children heard a "chick-a-dee-dee-dee." In a spruce tree sat a little black-capped bird waiting for some birdseed.

Becky ran inside to get some birdseed. When she came back, she held the birdseed out to the chickadee. It landed gently on her hand and picked out a large seed. Then it fluttered back to the spruce tree. "Chick-a-dee-dee-dee," it sang.

"Those chickadees are happy all the time," Becky said. "They never seem to grumble." She put some birdseed in the feeder. "When I see them singing in the snow, I feel like singing too."

"Me too," Mark said. "I think I'll try to be as cheerful as a chickadee."

"Cheerful Chickadees"

1. What details did you learn about chickadees?

2. How did God make chickadees to live in the cold weather?

3. What lesson did Mark and Becky learn from the chickadees?

4. Do you think God wants us to grumble or to be cheerful? Why?

Vocabulary

chuckled	twitter
ruffle	weather
tame	

Make Your Own Bird Feeder
illustrated by Kathy Pflug

1. Clean a milk carton.

2. Cut two openings.

3. Paint the outside of the milk carton.

4. Ask an adult to help you put a hook in the top.

5. Put birdseed inside the bird feeder and hang it outside near a window.

We Thank Thee

Now therefore, our God, we thank Thee, and praise Thy glorious name. - I Chronicles 29:13

Shelly Hamilton   Ron Hamilton

1. We thank Thee for the morn - ning light,
2. Our God is great, our God is good,
3. We thank Thee for the sum - mer breeze,

For rest and shel - ter through the night,
And we will thank Him as we should.
For song of birds, for shade of trees,

For health and food, for love and friends,
By His great hand we all are fed;
For stars that glit - ter in the sky,

For all Thy good - ness sends.
He gives our dai - ly bread.
We thank Thee, Lord on high.

A PROMISE TO REMEMBER

Drama by Dawn L. Watkins and Eileen M. Berry
illustrated by John Roberts

Cast

Mr. Allerton	Joseph Mullins
Mrs. Allerton	Sailor 1
Remember Allerton	Sailor 2
Mr. Mullins	Four friends
Mrs. Mullins	of Sailor 1

Act I

(Mr. and Mrs. Allerton and Mr. and Mrs. Mullins are sitting at a table. Remember and Joseph are playing in a corner.)

Mr. Allerton: We have to choose. The king has said we must go to his church. But we cannot go there and be true to our God.

Mr. Mullins: We can choose to obey the king, or we can choose to obey God.

Mrs. Allerton: It seems that there is just one thing to do.

Mrs. Mullins: That's true. We must do what God says. But we cannot stay here if we choose God's way.

Mrs. Allerton: Then it is settled? We will leave this land?

Mr. Allerton: Yes, we must sail to a new land. We must sail to America.

Mrs. Mullins: It will be hard to leave the friends we have met in this land.

Mrs. Allerton: Yes. And there is much to do. We will have to pack the things we will need in America.

Mr. Mullins: We must remember that God will take care of us. He will go with us.

Remember *(to Joseph)*: I wish we could stay.

Joseph: Why? It will be fun to ride on the *Mayflower*. Maybe we can even get out and ride in small boats sometimes.

Remember: I don't like small boats. They rock too much.

Joseph: We'll have lots of room to play in the new land. There will be no one there but us.

Remember: Mother says there will be Indians. I am afraid.

Joseph: The Indians will be our friends. We'll play with them. Just wait and see.

Mrs. Allerton: Come, Remember. We need to think about what to pack.

(Remember stands up and goes to the table.)

Mr. Allerton: One thing you will not need to take is your fear. Our God says, "I will never leave thee." Remember that.

Act II

(Remember and Mr. and Mrs. Allerton are standing at the rail of the ship. Sailor 1 is sitting off to one side of them, twisting some ropes.)

Remember: How much longer will we be on the *Mayflower*, Father?

Mr. Allerton: Many more days, Remember.

Sailor 1 *(mocking)*: Yes, many more days to be sick. Many more days to smell of fish and tar. Many more days for me to hear your silly stories of your God.

Mr. Allerton: We hope to reach America soon, sir. Then you will be rid of us.

Sailor 1: Ha, ha! That is true. Those of you who make it to America will soon die there. You will be tired and hungry. It will be too hard for you to live in a new land.

Remember *(whispering to Mr. Allerton)*: I wish that man would not make fun of us.

Mr. Allerton: It does not matter what he says. Remember what God says? "I will never leave thee." God is still with us.

Mrs. Allerton: Let's go to bed and get some rest.

(Mr. and Mrs. Allerton lie down. Sailor 1 leaves the stage.)

Remember *(kneeling)***:** God, please don't let us die like that man said. I am so afraid. Please take care of us.

(Remember lies down. Just before dawn, Joseph comes and shakes her.)

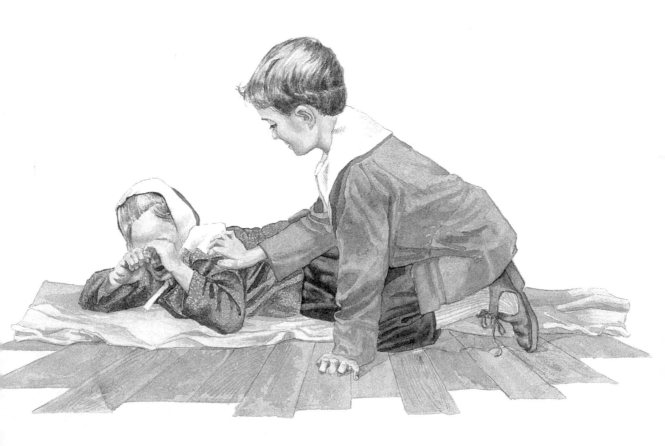

Joseph: Wake up, Remember! The sailors are going to throw a man off the ship.

Remember *(rubbing her eyes)*: Why?

Joseph: He got sick and died.

(Remember and Joseph watch four friends of Sailor 1 pass by, dragging Sailor 1 on a blanket.)

Remember *(whispering)*: Joseph! That's the sailor who made fun of us! He said we are all going to die.

Joseph: Yes. And now he is the one who died.

Remember: I think God is going to take care of us.

Joseph: I do too! Let's tell the others.

Act III

(Remember and Mrs. Allerton are sitting on deck.)

Remember: I feel so tired. So many are sick—even Joseph.

Mrs. Allerton: Yes. It has been a hard trip.

Remember: What if we never see land again? I don't want to die on this ship.

(Remember starts to cry softly. Mrs. Allerton hugs her gently.)

Mrs. Allerton: Let me tell you why your father and I named you Remember. We wanted you to remember that God is good. We wanted you to remember that God loves you and wants to help you. We wanted you to remember all of the things God has promised in the Bible.

Remember: Like "I will never leave thee"?

Mrs. Allerton: Yes, promises just like that one.

Remember (*still sniffling, but nodding*)**:** I will try to remember.

(Mrs. Allerton leaves. Mrs. Mullins comes to Remember.)

Mrs. Mullins: Remember! Here you are.

Remember: How is Joseph, Mrs. Mullins?

Mrs. Mullins: He is not very well. He wants you to come and see him.

(Remember and Mrs. Mullins go to Joseph, who is lying on a blanket. Remember kneels.)

Remember: I hope you are better soon, Joseph. I miss our games.

Joseph: Mother, do you think I'll get better?

Mrs. Mullins: I think so, Joseph. You need rest. If we can just reach land soon . . .

Remember: Don't be afraid, Joseph. Think about God. Remember, God will never leave you.

(In a corner, Sailor 2 steps up on a stool and shades his eyes with his hand.)

Sailor 2 *(very* excitedly*)*: Land ho!

(All Allertons and Mr. and Mrs. Mullins run to the rail. Joseph stands up and walks slowly to join them. Joseph and Remember are pointing.)

Mr. Mullins: There it is! America, our new home.

(All clap and cheer.)

Mr. Allerton: God keeps His promises. This is a day to remember.

"A Promise to Remember"

1. How many settings are in this drama? What are the settings?

2. Why did the Allerton family and the Mullins family get on the ship?

3. Do you think that the families made a wise choice? Why?

4. What important lesson did Remember learn?

Vocabulary

dawn	ha	settled
deck	mocking	sniffling

156

While Shepherds Watched Their Flocks by Night

WINCHESTER OLD

Nahum Tate   Este's *Psalter*

1. While shep - herds watched their flocks by night,
2. "Fear not!" said he, for might - y dread
3. "To you, in Da - vid's town, this day
4. "The heav'n - ly Babe you there shall find
5. Thus spake the ser - aph and forth - with
6. "All glo - ry be to God on high,

All seat - ed on the ground,
Had seized their trou - bled mind.
Is born of Da - vid's line
To hu - man view dis - played,
Ap - peared a shin - ing throng
And to the earth be peace;

The an - gel of the Lord came down,
"Glad tid - ings of great joy I bring
The Sav - iour Who is Christ the Lord,
All mean - ly wrapped in swad - dling bands,
Of an - gels prais - ing God on high,
Good will hence - forth from heav'n to men

And glo - ry shone a - round.
To you and all man - kind."
And this shall be the sign."
And in a man - ger laid."
Who thus ad - dressed their song:
Be - gin and nev - er cease."

157

The Puppy Who Wanted a Boy

Fantasy by Jane Thayer
illustrated by Lisa McCue

Think as You Read

Why does the puppy want a boy?

One day Petey, who was a puppy, said to his mother, who was a dog, "I'd like a boy for Christmas."

His mother, who was a dog, said she thought he could have a boy if he was a very good puppy.

So the day before Christmas Petey's mother asked, "Have you been a very good puppy?"

"Oh, yes!" said Petey. "I didn't frighten the cat."

"You didn't?" asked Petey's mother.

"Well-l, I just frightened her a *little*," said Petey. "And I didn't chew any shoes."

"Not *any*?" said his mother.

"Just a teeny-weeny chew," said Petey. "And I remembered—well, almost always remembered—to bark when I wanted to go out."

"All right," said his mother. "I think you've been good for such a little dog. I will go out and get you a boy for Christmas."

But when Petey's mother came back she
looked very worried. "How would you
like a soft white rabbit with
pink ears for Christmas?"
she said to Petey.

"No thanks," said Petey.

"Don't you want a lovely canary?"

"I'd like a boy," said Petey.

"How about some guppies?"
said Petey's mother.

"I just want a boy,"
said Petey.

162

"Petey," said his mother at last, "there are no boys to be found."

"No boys?" cried Petey.

"Not one could I find. They're terribly short of boys this year."

Petey thought he couldn't stand it if he didn't have a boy.

Finally his mother said, "There now, there must be a boy somewhere. Perhaps you could find some dog who would give his boy away."

"Do you think I could?" asked Petey.

"It wouldn't hurt to try," said his mother.

So Petey started off. It wasn't long before he saw a collie racing with a boy on a bicycle. Petey trembled with joy.

"If I had a boy on a bicycle," said Petey to himself, "I could run like anything! I'll take a little run right now, and I'll ask the collie politely if he'll give his boy away."

So Petey leaped after the bicycle. He called out
to the collie, "Excuse me. Do you want to give your
boy away?"

But the collie said no, he definitely didn't, in a
dreadful tone of voice.

Petey sat down. He watched the collie and his
boy on a bicycle, until they were out of sight.

"I didn't really want a boy on a bicycle, anyway,"
said Petey.

After a while he saw a setter playing ball with a boy. Petey was delighted. "If I had a boy to play ball with," said Petey, "I'd catch the ball smack in my mouth. I'd like to catch the ball now!"

But he remembered how cross the collie had been. So he sat down on the sidewalk and called out politely, "Excuse me. Do you want to give your boy away?"

But the setter said no, he definitely didn't, in a terrifying tone of voice!

"Oh, well," said Petey, trotting off, "I don't think playing ball is so much fun."

169

Soon Petey came to a bulldog, sitting in a car with a boy. Petey was pleased, for he was getting a little tired from so much walking.

"If I had a boy in a car," said Petey, "I'd laugh at walking dogs. I'd like a ride right now."

So he called out loudly, but very politely, "Excuse me. Do you want to give your boy away?"

But the bulldog said no, he definitely didn't, and he growled in Petey's face.

"Uh-oh!" said Petey. He hurried behind a house and stayed there until he saw the bulldog and his boy drive away.

"Well, who wants to go riding in a car? Not me!" said Petey, coming out from behind the house.

He thought he would just rest a while, though. He had come a long way for such a little dog. He was limping a bit when he started off again. After a while he met a Scottie, walking with his boy and carrying a package in his mouth.

"Now that is a good kind of boy!" said Petey. "If I had a boy to take walks with and carry packages for, there might be some dog biscuits or cookies in the package. I would like a cookie right now!" He hadn't had any lunch.

But he remembered how cross the collie and the setter and the bulldog had been. So he stayed across the street and shouted at the top of his lungs, but polite as could be, "Excuse me. Do you want to give your boy away?"

The Scottie had his mouth full with the package. But he managed to say no, he definitely didn't, and he showed his sharp teeth to Petey.

"I guess that wasn't the kind of boy I wanted either," said poor Petey. "But my goodness, where *can* I find a boy?"

Well, Petey trotted on and on. But he couldn't find a single dog who would give his boy away. Petey's ears began to droop. His tail grew limp. His little legs were *very* tired. My mother was right, he thought. There isn't a boy to be found.

Just as it was getting dark, he came to a large building on the very edge of town. Petey was walking by slowly when he saw a sign: HOME FOR BOYS.

"Maybe I could find a boy here!" said Petey to himself. "These boys have no parents, and no dog to take care of them either." He padded slowly up the walk of the Home. He was so tired he could hardly lift his little paws.

Then Petey stopped. He listened. He could hear music. He looked through the window. He saw a lighted Christmas tree, and children singing carols.

Then Petey saw something else. On the front
steps of the building, all by himself, sat a boy! He
was not a very big boy, and he looked lonely.

Petey gave a glad little cry. He forgot about being tired. He leaped up and landed in the boy's lap. Sniff, sniff, went Petey's little nose. Wag, wag, went Petey's tail. He kissed the little boy with his warm, wet tongue. How glad the boy was to see Petey! He put both his arms around the little dog and hugged him tight.

Then the front door opened and a lady looked out. "Why, here you are, Ricky!" she said. "What is our newest boy doing out here all alone? Come on in and sit near the Christmas tree."

Petey sat very still. The boy sat still. The boy looked up at the lady and down at Petey. Petey began to tremble. Would the boy go in and leave him?

"I'm not alone," said the boy, "I've got a puppy."

"A puppy!" The lady came out and looked at Petey in surprise.

"Can he come, too?" said the boy.

"Why," said the lady, "you're a nice little dog. Wherever did you come from? Yes, bring him in."

"Come on, puppy," cried the boy. In they scampered!

A crowd of boys was playing around the Christmas tree. They rushed at Petey. They picked him up and petted him.

Petey wagged his tail. He wagged his fat little body. He frisked about and licked every one of the boys.

185

"Can we keep him?" said one.

"Can we give him some supper?" said another.

"Can we fix him a nice warm bed?" said a third.

"We will give him some supper and a nice warm bed," said the lady. "And tomorrow we will find his mother and see if she'll let him stay."

Petey knew his mother would let him stay. She knew how much he wanted a boy. "But won't she be surprised," said Petey to himself, with a happy little grin, "when I tell her I got *fifty* boys for Christmas!"

The Puppy Who Wanted a Boy

1. Why did Petey want a boy?

2. What did Petey do to try to find a boy?

3. What gift did Petey receive? Do you think the gift was a special gift? Why?

4. Why do we give gifts at Christmas?

Vocabulary

biscuits	either	terribly
definitely	hardly	terrifying
delighted	managed	trembled
dreadful	politely	

189

The Promised Son

God made a promise when He said, *"I will give a Son to the woman."* The rest of the Bible tells how God kept His promise. As He had planned, God sent His Son. Jesus came to earth to die for the sin of all people.

Adam and Eve   Noah   Abraham

God Keeps His Promise

A Bible account taken from Matthew 1–2 and Luke 1–2 illustrated by Frank Ordaz

Think as You Read

How did God keep His promise to send His Son?

Moses	King David	The Birth of Jesus

The Son Is Born

One night Joseph had a dream. In his dream Joseph saw an angel. The angel of the Lord spoke to Joseph.

"God is doing something very special for Mary," the angel said. "God is giving Mary a Son. You are to take Mary to be your wife. And when the boy is born, you are to name him *Jesus*. He is the One who will save His people from their sins."

Joseph obeyed God, and Mary became his wife. Mary and Joseph went to Bethlehem. The baby was born in Bethlehem in a stable.

Angels gave praise to God. They told some shepherds in nearby fields that the Savior had been born. The shepherds went to Bethlehem. They saw the baby Jesus and Mary and Joseph in the stable. Then the shepherds gave praise to God. Jesus is the Son and Savior that God had promised!

After Jesus was born, wise men from the East came to Jerusalem. They came to talk to King Herod.

"Where is the child?" the wise men asked. "Where is the King of the Jews? We saw a star rise in the night sky. The star must mean that a great king has been born. We have come to worship Him."

When Herod heard what the wise men said, he was afraid. He called together people who studied the Scriptures.

"Where is this King to be born?" Herod asked the people.

"In Bethlehem," they replied. "God promised in the Scriptures that the great king from David's family would be born in Bethlehem."

"Go to Bethlehem," Herod told the wise men. "When you find the child, come back here and tell me. I want to worship him too."

God Protects His Son

The wise men left for Bethlehem. Then something amazing happened. They saw the star that they had seen when they were in the East. The star led the wise men right to the house where Jesus was staying. When they saw the star leading them, the wise men were filled with joy.

When the wise men entered the house, they saw Jesus with His mother, Mary. The wise men got down on their knees and worshiped the Son that God had sent into the world.

After the wise men worshiped Jesus, they gave Him three gifts. They gave Him gold, one of the most expensive metals in the world. They also gave Him frankincense, an expensive perfume used to worship God. Finally, they gave Him myrrh, a perfume that was sometimes put on a body before it was buried. Gold, frankincense, and myrrh were great gifts. They were gifts that would only be given to a great king.

When it was time for the wise men to leave, they planned to go back to Jerusalem. Herod had asked them to come back. But during the night God spoke to the wise men. "Do not go back to Herod," God told them. "You must go home another way." The wise men obeyed God.

Then God sent an angel to Joseph. In a dream, Joseph heard the angel of the Lord say, "You must leave Bethlehem. You must move to Egypt. Herod will try to kill the child." Joseph obeyed quickly.

Herod was very angry when he learned that the wise men had gone home another way. "I will find this new King and kill him," he said.

Herod sent soldiers to Bethlehem to find the new King. But the soldiers never found him. Jesus was safe with Mary and Joseph in the land of Egypt.

After a few years, God again sent an angel to speak to Joseph. "It is time to go home, Joseph," said the angel of the Lord. "Herod is dead. Take your family and go back to your own country. But do not go to Bethlehem. Go and live in the part of your country that is called Galilee."

Again Joseph obeyed God and moved his family to a town in Galilee. The name of the town was Nazareth. This town was Jesus' home for many years. Jesus grew up and became a man of great wisdom. People who watched Jesus carefully could tell that God had planned a great work for Jesus to do.

Jesus is the Son that God had promised in the Garden of Eden. Jesus was born to be the Savior of the world. Today, we can know that God always keeps His promises.

"God Keeps His Promise"

1. How is Jesus different from every other baby born?

2. What were some of the things that made Jesus' birth special?

3. God promised to send His Son. Did God keep His promise? Did God keep His promise right away?

4. Do you think that we can trust God to keep His promises?

Vocabulary

buried	myrrh	soldiers
expensive	praise	worship
frankincense	Savior	
metals	Scriptures	

Organizing Facts

A **word web** is used to organize information.
It helps us to remember facts that we read.

This word web is about gold. Facts that describe gold go
in the outer circles.

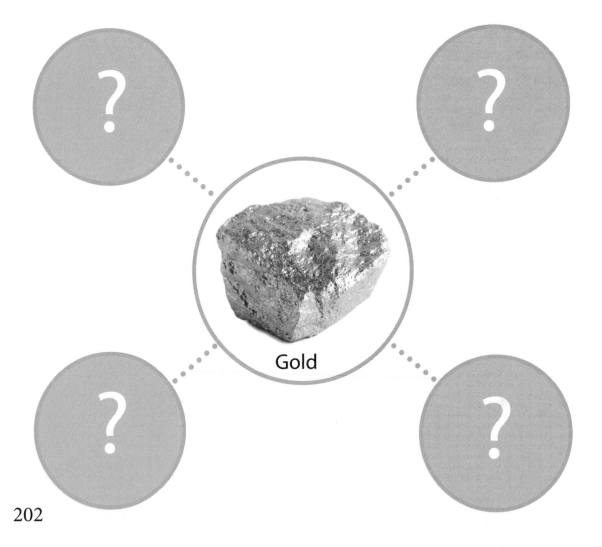

Gold

Gold, Frankincense, and Myrrh

*An article by
Eileen M. Berry
and Amy Schoneweis*

Think as You Read
What facts can I learn about the gifts
the wise men brought to Jesus?

Gold

Gold is a bright yellow metal. It is a beautiful metal that is hard to find. It does not rust, and it lasts a long time. Because gold is beautiful and lasts a long time, it is very expensive.

Gold can be molded into gold bars.

A pan can be used to find gold nuggets in creeks and streams.

Some people think that gold is found only in the ground. But gold can also be found in water. Pure gold is heavy, but it is very soft and easy to bend. Gold can be made into jewelry by mixing it with harder metals like copper or silver.

Kings have owned many gold things. The wise men made a good choice when they gave gold as a gift to Jesus. Gold is fit for kings, and Jesus is the King of Kings.

A crown is often made of gold.

Frankincense

Frankincense is sticky like tree sap. Pale yellow frankincense can be heated to make an oil. The oil has a sweet smell and is used to make perfume.

Frankincense trees have the sap for making perfume.

Frankincense comes out from a cut in the tree.

During Bible times, the perfume was burned for its sweet odor. The priests burned this perfume in the temple to worship God. The wise men's gift of frankincense was fitting for Jesus because He is the Son of God. One day everyone will worship Him.

Myrrh

Myrrh is also sticky like tree sap. Like frankincense, myrrh is used to make perfume. Myrrh can also be heated and cooled to make oil. People burn myrrh to smell its sweet odor.

During Bible times, myrrh was put on bodies before they were buried. When the wise men gave myrrh to Jesus, they made a good choice. One day Jesus would die for our sin. He would be buried, and He would rise from the dead.

Detail from *Adoration of the Magi* by Johann Boeckhorst, From the Bob Jones University Collection.

The wise men gave Jesus their finest gifts. What gift can you give Jesus? The finest gift you can give to Jesus is not gold or frankincense or myrrh. The finest gift is your heart—to love Jesus and to live for Him.

"Gold, Frankincense, and Myrrh"

1. Why is gold a special metal?

2. How are frankincense and myrrh alike? How are they different?

3. Why were gold, frankincense, and myrrh good gifts for the wise men to give to Jesus?

Vocabulary

heavy	odor	pure
jewelry	priests	sap

The Wise Men's Trip

A. Use the map to answer the question.

What do you think it was like for the wise men to travel all the way to Bethlehem?

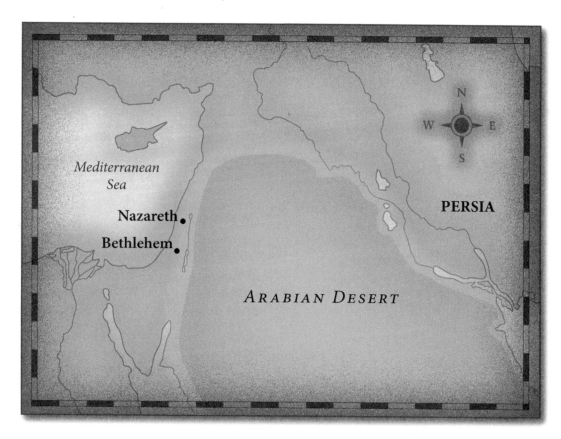

B. Pretend you are one of the wise men. On Worktext page 169, write a story about your trip. Tell which gift you would take to Jesus and why you would choose that gift.

USING A GLOSSARY

A **glossary** is a list of important or special words and their meanings. A glossary is found at the end of some books. Unlike a dictionary, a glossary contains only words that are used in the book.

This glossary has information about selected words in this reading book. It gives the meanings of these words that are used in some of the stories.

> The meaning of each entry word is given.

> Entry words are listed in alphabetical order.

> The syllables of an entry word are shown to help you read the word.

> A sample sentence helps you understand the word.

A

air—Different gases mixed together that you breathe. *The bird flew through the <u>air</u>.*

al·pha·bet—The letters used to write words. *Lucas can say all the letters of the <u>alphabet</u> from A to Z.*

alphabet

at·tic—A space or room just below the roof of a building. *Dad stores the Christmas decorations in the <u>attic</u>.*

B

blind—Not able to see. *The service dog led the <u>blind</u> boy across the street.*

bur·ied—To **bury** is to place in the ground. *The dog <u>buried</u> its bone in the backyard.*

C

car·a·mel—A chewy candy made from cooked sugar, butter, and milk. *Mother put melted <u>caramel</u> on top of the cake that she had baked.*

caramel

A

air—Different gases mixed together that you breathe. *The bird flew through the air.*

al·pha·bet—The letters used to write words. *Lucas can say all the letters of the alphabet from A to Z.*

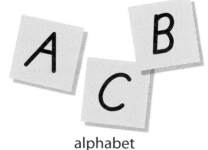

alphabet

at·tic—A space or room just below the roof of a building. *Dad stores the Christmas decorations in the attic.*

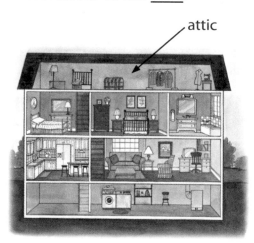

attic

B

blind—Not able to see. *The service dog led the blind boy across the street.*

bur·ied—To **bury** is to place in the ground. *The dog buried its bone in the backyard.*

C

car·a·mel—A chewy candy made from cooked sugar, butter, and milk. *Mother put melted caramel on top of the cake that she had baked.*

caramel

car·ried—To **carry** is to take from one place to another. *Dad carried baby Jacob into the house.*

chuck·led—A **chuckle** is a quiet laugh. *I chuckled when Emma told a funny story.*

com·pa·ny—Guests or visitors. *Mom made extra food to serve our company at dinner.*

coun·tries—A **country** is a land with its own people and laws. *England, Spain, and France are countries.*

D

deaf—Not able to hear, in part or at all. *Jesus healed a deaf man so that he could hear.*

de·ci·sion—A choice that is made after thinking about it. *Dad and Mom made a decision to buy a new van.*

des·sert—A sweet food that is usually eaten at the end of a meal. *We will have ice cream and cookies for dessert.*

dessert

E

else—Different; other. *My pen did not work, so I had to write with something else.*

ex·cite·ment—A feeling of joy or eager interest. *We showed our excitement by cheering at the game.*

ex·claimed—To **exclaim** is to suddenly cry out or speak loudly. *"She's here!" exclaimed Caleb when he saw Grandma getting out of her car.*

ex·pen·sive—Costs a lot of money. *Gold is very expensive.*

ex·plained—To **explain** is to tell about something in a way that is clear or easily understood. *The farmer explained why his land was good for growing corn.*

F

faint—To pass out or seem to suddenly fall asleep, usually for a short time. *Emma felt like she was going to <u>faint</u> when she saw the mouse.*

feath·ers—A **feather** is one of the light parts that grow from and cover the skin of a bird. *The bird's <u>feathers</u> help it to fly and keep it warm.*

feathers

few—Not many; a small number or amount. *Only a <u>few</u> people ran in the five-mile race.*

flut·tered—To **flutter** is to move with a quick and light flapping of the wings. *The butterfly <u>fluttered</u> above the flower.*

frank·in·cense—A sticky yellow liquid found in the sap or liquid from a special kind of tree. It has a sweet smell and can be used to make perfume. *The wise men gave <u>frankincense</u> to Jesus.*

freed—To **free** is to let go. *We <u>freed</u> the mouse from the trap.*

G

gi·ant—A person or thing that is very large and strong. *Molly read a story about a princess and a <u>giant</u>.*

H

hap·pi·ly—In a happy way. *I <u>happily</u> followed my brother into the ice-cream shop.*

heav·y—Having great weight. *I could not lift the <u>heavy</u> rock.*

I

i·de·a—A thought or a plan. *Mom's* idea *to go to the park after school was great.*

in·spect—To look at closely and carefully. *Miss James will* inspect *every part of the playground.*

in·ter·est·ed—To show **interest** is to be willing to do or learn something. *I asked Jack if he was* interested *in going to the zoo with me.*

J

jew·el·ry—Pretty objects such as necklaces and rings that are made to be worn. *My mom likes to wear* jewelry.

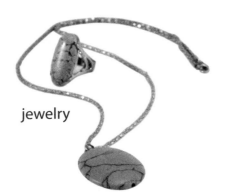

jewelry

K

L

lame—Not able to walk. *Jesus healed the* lame *man so that he could walk.*

M

met·als—**Metal** is something such as silver or gold that is usually shiny and hard. *A ring can be made from many different* metals.

mo·ment—A very short amount of time. *It will take only a* moment *to pick up that piece of trash.*

myrrh—A sticky brown liquid found in the sap or liquid from a special kind of tree. It has a strong smell and can be used to make perfume. *The wise men gave* myrrh *to Jesus.*

N

O

o·dor—A smell or scent. *Some kinds of perfume have a sweet odor.*

op·e·ra·tion—A way to treat a sickness or a hurt part of a person's body. *Jane must have an operation to fix her broken leg.*

P

phrase—A group of words that has meaning but is not a sentence. *"Mmm, mmm, good" is the phrase that Ann said in the play.*

pledge—A promise. *Mike made a pledge to clean his room after the baseball game.*

praise—To express the worth or value of something through words or songs. *When the shepherds saw the baby Jesus, they gave praise to God.*

pre·tend·ed—To **pretend** is to make believe. *Emily put on a fancy dress and pretended she was a princess.*

priests—In Bible times, a **priest** was a man who served God in the temple. *The priests led the Jews in worshiping God.*

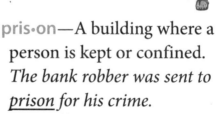

priest

pris·on—A building where a person is kept or confined. *The bank robber was sent to prison for his crime.*

prison

215

pro·tect—To keep safe from harm. *When riding my bike, I wear a helmet to protect my head.*

pure—Not mixed with anything else. *A ring that is made of pure gold costs a lot of money.*

Q

R

re·mem·bered—To **remember** is to think of again. *Seth remembered that he needed insects for his science project.*

re·plied—To **reply** is to give an answer. *When Mom asked a question, I replied quickly.*

ruf·fle—To move or lift something so that it is not smooth. *Our pet bird started to ruffle his feathers when he saw the cat.*

S

sal·sa—A spicy sauce made from tomatoes, onions, and peppers. *A topping for the tacos is salsa.*

salsa

sap—The liquid that flows through a plant. *Maple syrup is made from the sap of maple trees.*

Sa·vior—The Lord Jesus Christ who saves people from sin. *Jesus, God's Son, is the promised Savior.*

scam·per—To run or move quickly. *I had never seen him scamper so fast.*

scram·bled—To **scramble** is to move quickly, often by climbing or crawling. *Our cat scrambled up a tree.*

Scrip·tures—The writings of God; the Bible. *We read in the Scriptures that Jesus was born in Bethlehem.*

Scriptures

scur·ried—To **scurry** is to move with light, quick steps. *I grabbed the cloth and scurried back to the ladder.*

sew·ing—To **sew** is to make or fasten together using a needle and thread. *Macie's mom is sewing a new dress.*

shad·ow—A dark shape or shade that forms when something blocks light. *Mia rested in the shadow of a tree.*

shrieked—To **shriek** is to make a loud, shrill cry. *The children shrieked when they saw the snake.*

so·fa—A long seat with a back and arms. *Four children can sit on the sofa in our living room.*

sofa

sol·diers—A **soldier** is a person who serves in an army. *The soldiers that just returned from the war will march in the parade.*

soldier

Span·ish—Having to do with Spain, its people, or its language. *Jon's class sang "Jesus Loves Me" in Spanish.*

squint·ed—To **squint** is to look with the eyes partly closed. *Abby squinted when she tried to read the tiny words.*

strange—Not usual; different. *Kyle was not sure if he wanted to eat the strange food on his plate.*

swol·len—Larger than the usual size because of a sickness or being hurt. *Jan's swollen foot would not fit into her shoe.*

T

ta·cos—A **taco** is a corn tortilla folded around a filling such as meat or cheese. *Jason likes to eat his tacos with hot sauce.*

taco

tame—Gentle and not afraid. *After a few months, the wild birds became tame.*

taught—The past tense of **teach**, to help someone learn. *I was taught to read when I was five years old.*

threw—The past tense of **throw**, to send something through the air with a quick movement of the arm. *James threw the ball to me, and I caught it.*

tor·til·las—A **tortilla** is a thin, round Mexican bread made from cornmeal or wheat. *Mom made the tortillas for our tacos.*

tortilla

twit·ter—To make repeated light chirping sounds. *The birds began to twitter softly as I walked through the woods.*

U

un·der·neath—Below or under. *Owen found a worm underneath that large rock.*

V

W

weath·er—What the air outside is like, such as rainy or cold. *God protects wild birds from the cold weather.*

whis·pered—To **whisper** is to speak softly or quietly. *Anna whispered to her mother in church.*

whist·led—To **whistle** is to make a high sound by blowing air through the lips or teeth. *Carlos whistled for his dog to come.*

wor·ship—To show love, honor, and respect. *We worship God in church.*

X

Y

Z

PHOTO CREDITS